*HIS

For I am His and He is Mine

Kayla Simmons

Fulton Books
Meadville, PA

Published by Fulton Books 2023

ISBN 978-1-64952-212-2 (paperback)
ISBN 978-1-64952-213-9 (digital)

Printed in the United States of America

This book is dedicated to my mother and father, Tahriq and Jenny Baker, as well as my family and everyone who fed into my life.

Imagine belonging to someone who's the most renounced in the world, and they could give you everything you ever wanted or asked for. That would be quiet amazing, wouldn't it? Well, being *His as in God's goes far beyond that, for He is the great God and can give you way more than man could. In today's world of social media, texting, and e-mailing, many get used to the rapid responses that it creates. However, with the rapid response errors are often made, therefore, a quick fix is simply when something has been spelled incorrectly, the wrong punctuation, or improper capitalization, you put an asterisk and then rewrite it correctly. By adding the asterisk, it's a neat fix that is used often in this technology-savvy generation. With that said, lately on social media and particularly on Twitter, I've noticed that the emphasis of the proper capitalization wasn't being applied when referring to God and Jesus. I then sent out a tweet, saying, "It's *God, not god," and that's when it all started. Psalm 95:3 states, "For the Lord is the great God, the great King above all gods." In all we do, we must respect God and have reverence for His name. This book is about being His in every aspect of your life, for we are *His and He is ours.

The Preparation

I was born a Navy brat in 1994 in Portsmouth, Virginia, with everything ahead of me. Before I was even able to comprehend life, I was destined for a life quite different from most. I spent most of my early life not fitting in and battling between trying to fit in and embracing the fact that I was set apart. I went from nodding my head in the back seat to "Da Brat" to at the age of four, quoting scriptures from the Bible. I guess one could say that God took my life for a turn indeed; however, it wasn't and won't be easy. From that age on, I knew I was in this world but not of it.

However, a moment where it hit me was when I was in the third grade, and my parents were teaching my siblings and me about the root of Halloween. Therefore, when the school had a Halloween parade, I couldn't participate. I remember having to wait until the "hallelujah" party at church that night. I'm pretty sure those who grew up in the church can relate. It was myself and about four other students from the entire school that was separated to watch a movie and eat treats. This effort was so we wouldn't be stuck doing work while everyone else was having fun. I remember crying at that moment because all my friends, along with other kids from my church, were outside having fun, but I wasn't. As I sat there and tears ran down my face, I felt alone because, in fact, I was alone. However, I understood why I couldn't go, but I still didn't like the left out feeling that I felt inside. I knew it was the "principle," something my parents preached to us for years prior, leading up to that point. Yet at such an early age, I didn't understand that I was being shaped and molded by God. I didn't understand that later in life, I'd look back and understand that very lesson. Most importantly, I didn't understand that there would be an array of similar scenarios to follow. Throughout that time, I was indeed being trained on how to be strong. We usually don't realize that we're in vigorous training by God until after the fact.

One example of this is when my brothers were babies, my father would lay my brothers on their backs, and he'd get a co-hanger and grab their small fingers and make them grip onto the hanger. It sounds silly, but as they'd grip onto it, my dad would gently pull the hanger, which would cause them to do baby versions of bench presses. At first, they couldn't do it; however, over time, with age and repetition, they had the strength to do it. That's what God does in our lives. He gives us just what we can handle for the time being as He's also strengthening us for the road ahead. God knows the beginning from the end, and He knows exactly what we can handle and what we need. More shall not be placed on us than that which we can bare, Corinthians 10:13.

I'm pretty sure we all can look back on our lives and realize times at which we were fully prepared for something due to our preparation. Imagine, on the other hand, if you walked into a classroom, and you were completely unprepared. You didn't have a pencil, knowledge of the material, or anything needed to be successful. You walked in simply blinded. If that was the case, you'd be unprepared and most likely would fail the test. Preparation, therefore, is defined as the action or process of making ready or being made ready for use. God is preparing you to be used by Him, and He's making provisions for you along the way. He wants us to succeed, but we must allow God to mold and to shape us. Through this, our job is to not get stuck in the lessons, and to do that, we can't get frustrated in what God is trying to get us to learn that we quit and give up in the middle of the lesson plan. The "lessons" and the "homework" prepare you for the test ahead; therefore, we must do a better job of being patient and showing God that we trust Him. Just as the reward you get from passing a test is a good grade, God's reward is you get closer to your purpose after each trial you overcome.

One of my trials in my early years was I typically felt isolated. This usually left me battling between trying to fit in or not. During that time of my life, I didn't fully understand that God was keeping me for a "divine" purpose, for most children wouldn't fully grasp it.

It wasn't until years later that I understood my purpose and then stopped trying so hard to fit in and embraced everything that was different about me. I will be the first to tell you that it's trying, emotional, lonely, difficult, and indeed a battle—yet worth it a thousand times. As a Christian, if you're going through a period where you're feeling isolated, it's because you're trying to do what's right by abiding by God's word. The isolation comes into play because those around you are most likely not living a God-fearing lifestyle and abiding by His words. That's where the struggle comes in to play. You're trying to align with God's trajectory for your life. Through this, a key word that I previously stated was "worth." God's word will always be worth standing alone. God's word is always worth going against the crowd. God's word indeed is worth everything. Yet we have to remember that He is Abba. We call God Abba because He is our Father. He is there for us to hold us and make us feel safe and secure in Him even when we're feeling isolated by the world.

One morning, I was watching a sermon on YouTube, and the word "*buck*" dropped in my spirit. Shortly after, the acronym came to me, "Being Uniquely Created for the Kingdom." I love that because that's exactly what's going on. We're "being" uniquely created for the kingdom because it's continuous. It's not an easy thing having to "*buck*" against everything in this world, but God is on our side. Our heavenly Father is there for us. However, a practical thing you can do during the times of feeling isolated is surround yourself with like-minded people, as staying in your word. This doesn't mean you cut off all your old friends and go handpick what you'd think was the "perfect" Christians and force a friendship—no, not at all. I am saying be aware of those around you and identify if those relationships are pulling you down or lifting you up and move accordingly. If we really begin to understand the word "His," we will have a distinct perspective on what it means to be a Christian, and as a result, it will help with the struggles we may have. By saying I am His, you are saying you belong to God. For I am His and He is mine. So when you're struggling with your individual identity in Christ, remind yourself that you have to *buck* every day in this walk with Christ.

A simple comparison would be one to a relationship—for a relationship, you represent one another. Representing one another is the same principle in our walk with God. We are representations of Christ, and we should live in such a way that people can see Christ in us. I once had a dream, and I know it was a dream that was sent straight from God, and I believe it's a message as well as a motto believers should live by. So in the dream, I was sitting at a desk in a classroom all alone, and God's voice was in the room, and He was speaking to me. As He was speaking to me, I was writing everything He said down. During that time, He was revealing my sins to me and, in a way, giving me the rundown of what I needed to work on. The voice then spoke with more authority and proceeded to say, "Be a good representation of my word." I immediately wrote it down on the paper. All you could see was my handwriting it on to the paper. Those words were spoken with so much power and authority that after I wrote it down in the dream, it immediately woke me out of my sleep.

Now let me explain something. When you stare at something for a long time and then you look away and you can still see somewhat of blotches of the light or the image itself, that's called an afterimage. Afterimage is when an image continues to appear after the exposure to the original image has ceased. That occurred as soon as I woke up, and my heart was beating extremely fast, and I was facing my wall. As I looked at my wall, my handwriting from me writing, "Be a good representation of His word," was on my wall like an afterimage. Mind you, I was no longer dreaming. I sat up, rubbed my eyes, looked at the wall again, and it was still there! At that moment, I just knew I was going crazy, so I then googled "Be a good representation of His word" because I was sure it had to be a scripture. It wasn't. It was around 3:00 a.m., and I put it in my notes on my phone because I believed God was trying to tell me something.

As Christians, I believe we are called to be exactly that good representations of His word. Representation is defined as the action of speaking or acting on behalf of someone or the state of being so represented. That is exactly what we, as Christians, are charged to do. Every day that we have breath on this earth, we are representing

Christ and what we say we believe, which is ultimately His word. For we are *His, and we represent Him. The dynamic of us being *His is like that of an actual relationship because you represent one another, and you can't belong to them and someone else and be in congruence. That would be called cheating, and in our relationship with God, that would be called lukewarm. Revelation 3:16 says, "So because you are lukewarm and neither hot nor cold, I will spit you out of my mouth." We cannot be *His and the worlds. You're either hot or cold, for Him or against Him.

One afternoon that ended up playing out in the car one day. We were heading home from getting some food, and the whole family was in the car. I was extremely hot. I felt like I was sweating bullets. Therefore, I yelled out from the back seat, "I'm hot! Can someone please cut the air on?" Little did I know they'd do just that. The air was blasting, and within ten minutes, I was shivering. Without even thinking that I just blurted out one request, I blurted out another, "I'm freezing!" My father then responded to me in a very fed up tone, asking me if I was hot or cold. Thinking back on this story, I realize that I was actually one more than the other. This leads me to understand that the life that you live reflects what your true choice is. For your mouth sings the music, but your actions bleed ears with the truth. What are your actions saying? We must make sure that our actions line up with His word and what we say we believe. Though I was cold after the air was turned on, I was truly hotter than I was cold. We have to learn to be true representations of Christ.

Shopping Cart

Real-life scenarios have been some of the greatest demonstrations in my life of God's word, and if you sit back and watch, you can see things in a new light. I remember a time when I was at work, and a lady said something that changed my perspective on the unnecessary things that we do in life. I was working at Publix Supermarkets at the time, and this customer who was a regular saw me outside pushing carts up to the building. I noticed that she saw me, and she yelled for me across the parking lot. I thought she was just saying hello, so I yelled back and said hello! She then waved me down to go to her, so I went ahead and walked her way. The lady had a box of kitty litter that she was returning, and she wanted me to take it out of her trunk and place it in the cart that I had and take it to customer service. So at that moment, I was thinking in my head, *I know she didn't call me overall so she can be lazy.* However, I told her I'd just carry it after we get in the store because I was going to put the cart up once we got in. She responded to me by saying, "No, that's 'unnecessary,' and you don't have to do the unnecessary carrying."

This story is relevant because a lot of times in life, we do the "unnecessary" carrying, not realizing who we are and whose we are. Psalm 55:22 says, "Turn your burdens over to the Lord, and he will take care of you. He will never let the righteous person stumble." The Bible also speaks of heavy burdens in Matthew 11:28, saying, "Come to me all who are weary and heavy-laden, and I will give you rest." The question then becomes, Why do we choose the unnecessary route? Why don't we call out to God to bring the "shopping cart" to carry our burdens? If we say we believe in God and we call ourselves His, we have the privilege to give our burdens over. That is why we praise Him because we know that we are not deserving of such. I think what we as Christians should take away from the older lady is that we don't have to do this alone. We are *His, and we are to place our burdens in the "shopping cart," for we don't have to carry the weight of our worlds.

Imagine if you were leaving a grocery store, and you saw someone carrying twenty-plus grocery bags. They had plenty up their arms, some around their neck, some tucked under their arms, just grocery bags everywhere. Then you walked up and offered them a grocery cart, and they say to you, "I can carry this alone. I got this." That's how we look sometimes. We have to realize that the shopping cart is free. Jesus Christ has already paid the cost, so we are blessed to be able to give our burdens over to God. Don't deny the shopping cart. We don't have to do the unnecessary carrying. God does this because He loves us so. Our human minds cannot even begin to fathom this kind of love, for this is the same kind of love that led Jesus to die on the cross for our sins. Imagine something so precious and costly being handed to you, and you just ignore it. That's what we do when we don't place our burdens in the "shopping cart." It's never a good thing to witness someone ignoring something special.

I got a chance to witness something precious being ignored at work one evening. On this particular day at Publix, I was checking a lady out, and she was with her son who was about five years old. The lady was talking to me about her groceries and some coupons. It really wasn't important. As she was telling me this, her son was doing everything he could to get her attention. The boy was tapping her and calling her "Mommy." She continued to ignore him as he cried. He then said this one thing that caught me and the mother's attention immediately. This five-year-old said, "What is so important that you ignore me?" That was a powerful thing that the little boy said. The mother then dropped down in a squat and was eye level with the little boy. She then said, "You are the most important thing in my life. I was just distracted." The mother's response was powerful as well, and in that moment, I wanted to drop my mouth and stare in awe of what God was showing me. That's how God looks at us sometimes. "What's so important that you ignore me?"

The Bible says that God is a jealous God; therefore, He longs for our attention (Exodus 34:14) The crazy part is God is the best thing that will ever happen to us. For we are a product of His love, and if anyone is ignored, God is the last one deserving of it. Just as the mother got distracted, we get distracted sometimes and ignore the most important thing in our life. We must begin to set time aside and let God know He's the best thing that ever happened to us. Hopefully, this will encourage you to "drop to your knees" and acknowledge to God that He's the best thing that's ever happened to you and that sometimes you get distracted. Take a moment to acknowledge Him as the most important.

Fences

Growing up as a child, I guess one would say I lived the "ideal" childhood. As an adult now, I don't have to heal from my childhood, which is simply a blessing. Your childhood is your formative years, which is what makes you who you are as an adult. Those years have such a strong influence on the rest of your life moving forward, which makes it vital in a person. It didn't take me long at all for me to realize that God was in control and that he had a "system" set in place to keep me throughout my years. My father would always use the analogy of a puppy, which I truly despised at the time. He would begin to explain to us that a newborn puppy doesn't want any boundaries or rules; however, it doesn't understand the safety in the fence. He'd explain that on the other side of the fence is a highway, a huge dog, the woods, a ditch, the lake, and other unknown dangers. The dog, however, is incapable of seeing that because of the level of maturity he has as a puppy. Yet it's the owner's job to protect the puppy from what it doesn't know even if it hurts the puppy in a way—its feelings.

It's foolish to want freedom behind the fence if you're incapable of seeing what it's blocking you from. With that said, living within the fence was my childhood, and it was hard at times, but I was being protected. I think every good parent tries to protect their child from "beyond the fence," but I'd like to say my parents had a concertina wire fence. Those fences are typically used at prisons or for military purposes because it understands what's within the fence. A prison must use those kinds of fences because it understands the danger it holds within, and it's protecting the outside world from within the fence. On the other hand, the military personnel uses the fences because they understand the value that they have within the fence, and they are guarding the valuable while it's vulnerable and in training. That's the same thing that God does for us. He puts fences around us and sets us apart because He understands the "training" that must take place, along with the value that we have within the fence.

Do you get frustrated within the fence not understanding that you're in training and you're vulnerable? I think we all do, for the fence principle goes way beyond the dynamic between a parent and a child. It's a representation of setting boundaries and protection around you for a greater purpose. As a society, we don't like boundaries or rules, when indeed they should be foundational things in our lives—especially Christians. Therefore, we must begin to understand how to put up the proper fences that we may need for that specific time in our life.

I personally got all too familiar with having boundaries when I went off to college. "Mommy and Daddy" weren't going to be there forever to put up the fences and create boundaries and safe grounds for me while I was away. I remember growing up, my parents would tell us that our grandparents would tell them to know God for yourself, and that's something they would tell us growing up as well. However, I didn't completely understand and grasp what that really meant until I went to college. Yes, we were going to a Christian college, but you can't be naive and think that it was going to be all petals and roses. It was definitely better than a public institution, but it wasn't a perfect environment. The same day my parents left, I felt exposed. I felt exposed simply by the fact that there were no boundaries. Therefore, I had to create those boundaries of things that I wouldn't do and what I wouldn't allow in my life. It's very difficult living with boundaries; however, it's even more difficult having to transform your life and create boundaries for yourself that you have to abide by. This, however, is vital in your walk with Christ because it teaches you discipline, for discipline is the first step to learning how to kill your flesh daily. It was crucial for me to set those boundaries within my life because if not, I was potentially setting myself up to be running riot. I believe one of the last places one needs to be running riot at is college; however, that's where most tend to run riot at. The reason for it is simply because those boundaries are no longer up like they probably were before because they were forced to abide.

After a few days of living in Florida away from my parents and their rules, I realized that I had to utilize what had been placed in me, which was my morals and what I believed in. I had to put up fences because I no longer wanted to feel vulnerable to everything that the world could've potentially thrown at me. When you don't live with boundaries, you are living a very dangerous life. Therefore, we must understand our value and put up those concertina wire fences because everything and everyone shouldn't have access to you. So if you feel like your life is completely exposed, it's okay—just start the process of putting up the fence and protecting yourself with boundaries. Understanding yourself and knowing what you stand for will help make your fence a strong and sturdy standing fence. I know you're probably thinking how do I turn my life from running riot to disciplining myself and putting up fences to create boundaries in my life. One thing for sure is it's not easy, and you'll need to always keep that you're *His at the forefront of your mind.

When you truly begin to understand that you're *His, it'll make it a little easier to create those boundaries in your life. I don't have all the answers, and my job as a believer is to always point you to God because, as I was taught by my parents, He is the source, not me. But with that said, I do have a few questions for you to ask yourself that might be able to assist you.

1. First step, what's your why? Why do you want these boundaries in your life?
2. Second, what areas of your life do you need more boundaries? You'll need to evaluate those areas of your life that you feel like are exposed to the outside world or "beyond the fence."
3. Third, begin to create a line between you and the world. Boundaries mark a limit of an area. It's basically a dividing line. Therefore, it's a separation from you and the world. "For we are in this world but not of this world." What's separating you?

If we are truly *His, there should be a clear difference in the way that we live our lives and the way that we do things. Our lives should stand for something different. Back in, I believe, 2007, I got in the car one day from school, and I was in about the seventh grade at the time. When I got in the car with my sister, the whole family was in the car, and I began to complain and express the need for some new shoes. I believed that my shoes were old and kind of dirty, so I went on this long-detailed explanation as to why my parents needed to buy me some new ones (they were unmoved). I felt like I didn't fit in because my shoes weren't super clean or new. My little brother, who was probably six or seven at the time, then yelled out, "Somebody gotta be different!" Everyone in the car fell out laughing beside me, of course, because it wasn't funny at the time at all. I say that story to say, "Somebody gotta be different." That's what we're called to. We are supposed to be different as Christians. Therefore, it's okay if you feel like you're somewhat isolated, for we are a chosen people. We are to be the light of the world, the city on a hill. So I charge you to put fences around your life to create those boundaries and live a different lifestyle, for "somebody gotta be different," and that somebody is you. This, in fact, should excite you that you are a different person.

The Bible says in 1 Peter 2:9, "You are a chosen people, a royal priesthood, a holy nation, God's special possession, that you may declare the praises of Him who called you out of the darkness into His wonderful light." Who wouldn't want to be in God's wonderful light? Who wouldn't want to be God's special possession? Who wouldn't want to be a part of a holy nation and a royal priesthood? Lastly, who wouldn't want to be a chosen people? I think we'd all agree that we'd like to be included in that. However, it calls for us to be obedient and different, for "somebody gotta be different." Being a "different" people isn't just about being at a place where we're close to God. It's about being that light and that city on a hill that is mentioned in 1 Peter 2:9. In being that light and the city on a hill, you are "different" but not just different in a peculiar kind of way. You're different for a reason—purposefully different.

When I was younger, I was such a nosy kid. I watched people around me and their actions all the time. By me doing so, it ended up influencing my life and impacting my worldview. One person, in particular, was my mother. I watched everything that she did, along with trying to mimic her as well. I remember one time specifically, I was in the second grade, and we had a babysitter come over, and she watched my siblings and me. Well, she began to prepare our food so we could eat, and she wasn't doing it the way my mother would have. Therefore, I thought I'd let her know (that was a mistake). I told her, "That's not how my mother does it," and her response to me was "Well, I'm not your mother." As I look back on it now, the story makes me laugh to think that I said that, and even more, her response was epic. I told this story to paint a picture of how well I knew my mother because of time spent and observation. There's no way I'd know her ways just by coincidence, for my life was intentional. I intentionally watched her every move because I admired her deeply. I knew her so well that when someone temporarily stepped into her role and wasn't representing what she'd do, I couldn't help but "try" to bring correction. Do you know God in that way?

Do you admire God?

Do you know His ways?

Do you know what's not God?

Are you truly His?

These are questions you should begin to ask yourself. In order for you to be able to rightfully answer these questions, you would have to truly know God. As Christians, we are to seek God to know God. In 1 Chronicles 16:11, it says, "Seek the Lord and His strength; seek His face continually." Therefore, that's repetitive and intentional doings. If it's impossible for us as humans to truly know one another off one conversation, it's impossible for us to know God the creator by occasionally getting to know Him. We must seek Him. For we are *His, and He is ours. Therefore, we must truly seek to know every aspect of who we serve. Though we will never understand God completely, we can still continuously seek His face, and as we do that, new things will begin to be revealed to us.

I've said for I am His and He is mine multiple times, but do we truly walk in that? "His" can be simply defined as belonging. Belonging can be defined as the property of or as a member or a part of something or someone. Therefore, when we say we are God's, we are saying we belong to God, as in His property, a part of Him, and a member. Meaning, we should reflect that we are a part of Him with the way that we live our lives daily. Without question, we are *His; however, the questions that you should begin to find answers to are, "Is He yours? Is God vital to your being? Do you go days without talking to Him? In every way, do you acknowledge Him? Does your life reflect one of a righteous lifestyle?" If you didn't answer all those questions with a yes, it's okay. The first step is recognizing where growth is needed. The next step is watering where you know growth is needed. In order to get your relationship where you want it, it's going to take intentional doings and honest love for God.

You're probably thinking, *How can I get love for God?* That's something that should be automatic. Well, understanding the heart of God and His love for us will be the first start of loving an amazing God or increasing your love for Him. In order for this, we must give our hearts to God. Proverbs 23:26 says, "My son, give me your heart and let your eyes delight in my ways." Once we truly understand God's heart and we give our hearts to Him, we will be able to delight in His ways. Once we begin to delight in His ways, we will begin to understand life even more within the fence. The fence won't be limited to boundaries, for it'll be a result of living life in a way that reflects the heart of God. So don't look at the fence like it's such a dreadful thing. Look at it as a great head of protection to get you closer to God.

Have you ever had a moment where you felt so close to God, but you just wanted to sit there? Were you in such a place where you didn't want to move that you wanted to live right there in His presence? If you haven't, you will experience it eventually, and it will be the most fulfilling thing you'll ever experience. As Christians, we must desire His presence like that. I once sent out a tweet that almost sent Twitter in a pandemonium. The tweet said, "If you have no desire to be in God's presence here on earth, why do you desire heaven?" The conundrum question left many pondering and others having epiphanies. The question simply challenges the process in which one thinks about heaven. If you simply want to go to heaven because you don't want to go to hell, I believe you're missing it. We should desire heaven because we desire a greater level of His presence. Therefore, while we're still here on earth, we should desire to have His presence here as well. So ask yourself, "Do I desire His presence?" For I am His and He is mine, and we should desire deeply to rest in God's presence.

Growing up, I'd hear songs as well as here people talk about how in His presence is where they wanted to be. At the time though, I thought I understood but in actuality, not quite. It's similar once again to the dynamic of a relationship. When it's good or when it's bad, you usually want to be in joined presence with your significant other. This is because no matter what happens, love overrules it all. Therefore, God's presence and His love conquer all. In His presence is where we should long to be. Having a relationship with Christ isn't something that you'll have within a snap of a finger. No, it's something you'll need to search out. You will find Him when you seek Him. I remember as a child, I would ask my father a question, and he'd usually say the same thing each time. My father would say, "Go look it up in the encyclopedia." For those who are unsure, that was basically the Internet before the Internet. I remember hating that response as a child because I just wanted him to give me the answer I was looking for. I simply didn't want to do the work. In that, my father was teaching us how to seek out what we were looking for. So there were plenty of times where he'd say, "Look it up," and I wouldn't because I didn't care that much to know. Do you care that much about your relationship with God, or do you give up when it calls for seeking on your part? One thing for sure is when I did go look for the answer in the encyclopedia, I knew that if I looked hard enough and long enough, I'd find what I went searching for. Therefore, we will find God if we truly seek Him.

I began writing this book in 2016, and it is now 2020, and I've been married for almost two months. The process of being engaged and now married has been extremely difficult, but most of that is for another book! However, the one area I do want to touch on which pertains to seeking God and you will find God is when I first moved to Jacksonville after the wedding. For the first few weeks, my relationship with God was a little rocky. I was having trouble hearing from God. Honestly, I remember being in the shower one day, weeping because I felt like God left me. Obviously, that wasn't true. I entered into a new chapter in my life, and it called for me to go higher in Him. Therefore, I had to seek Him vigorously. I didn't at first. I sat in my feelings, and I went through the motions because things changed. I would send up a prayer here and there, cut on some worship music here and there. But I knew I wasn't seeking Him. I truly hit rock bottom. Then it clicked for me. God was the same God He's always been. I am the one who stopped going to the encyclopedia. I wanted someone to give me the answer, and I forgot that I built my relationship with God by seeking God. So enough with the excuses. It's time to get serious about seeking out the creator. For I am His and He is mine.

Missing God

In our world today, it's extremely hard to be physically alone. If you don't live with others, you work with people, shop with people, or go to church with people. In proximity, there are always people. Now how is it that at times we may feel alone? This, in fact, is because we may be surrounded physically, but spiritually, you can feel alone. Yet, God, as we know, never leaves or forsakes us. The question is, Are we the same way? At times, we can be the one who turns our backs to God and block Him out. With that, do you feel yourself drifting away from God? Are you trying to reel yourself back in? Why do you feel alone? I personally find myself in that situation sometimes—missing God.

When I was a little girl, my parents thought it was hilarious because I always wanted to go down memory lane. I'd always reminisce on what we all call the "good ole days." It's crazy because sometimes you can find yourself looking back on the "good ole days" with God and wondering what happened. So what happened? Why are you in a state of missing God? One of the reasons someone misses one is because they miss their presence or their company. I know for me personally when I felt like I was far away from God or drifted off from my relationship. One of the things I missed the most was His presence and His company. In life, when you're going through challenging times in your life, you like to be in the presence or in the company of loved ones or friends. This is not because they can fix your problems but simply because you value their presence. Loved ones provide comforting company. Now imagine going through these same situations and having God Himself walking with you and holding your hand. I think, if we take the time to think about it, we'd be overwhelmed by that very thought. However, as you begin to drift so far away from God, it's not that He's no longer there. In fact, it's a matter of being so far or so deep in sin that you can't "feel" His presence or company at the time. This then equates to you missing God's presence.

Another reason one may miss someone is that they miss the memories. Do you miss the memories with God? You're probably thinking about what memories do I have with God. Well, I'm talking about what God has done for you. Those things that you look back on and remember how He got you out of a situation. These are the memories of His works and wonders in your life. When we've strayed away from God, it can be hard to see the works of God's hand in our life; therefore, we begin to miss the memories. Also, when missing someone, we tend to miss their love, friendship, and connection the most. This is something that's vital in any relationship, including one with God. You must get back to a place where you're close to God and living your day-to-day life being able to see His works and provisions.

So you miss God, what now? Well, your relationship with God obviously changed, yet He remained the same. Therefore, you must get back in the right standings with Him. This means you must honestly evaluate yourself and ask, "Was I just using God?" Were you in pursuit of a relationship with Him just because you wanted the benefits? Yes, the benefits of being in a relationship with God is amazing. However, we must seek God for God. The great part is the benefits will come regardless, yet we still must do a heart check. If we're only in it for the benefits, that could be what makes it easy for us to stray away when it gets tough or even when it gets good. One thing you don't want to do is treat God like an option. God is and will always be the answer.

Now let's take a moment to acknowledge how good God is despite how we may treat Him sometimes. Even when we ignore God or turn our backs to Him, He still provides for us, blesses us, and keeps us on His mind. Who do you know that will do that? Also, one willing to accept you back at any time? That's why we praise His name because He's a good father. It's ludicrous because, as humans, we don't half love our families. We love our families through their good and their bad. Yet, at times, we display half love for God. Now mind you, this is a God that has no bad. This is a God that only requires us to give up ourselves and put Him first. This is a God that sent His only begotten son for us. This is that God. We need to get to a place where our hearts are completely His. He truly doesn't deserve to be half loved. One thing that's for sure is when you've strayed away from God, your light seems to be a little dimmer—as your light is not shining as bright as it once was before. Therefore, sometimes when you've "backslid," it can be hard to recognize yourself. However, as Christians, we are expected to be a certain way, for people are always watching. Yes, we make mistakes at times, but we need to get back to God.

Getting back to God can be a challenge, but what's indeed harder than falling is staying strong and standing tall. I remember as a child, I would get upset at times because I felt like I didn't have a "story." What I was unaware of was that it's harder to keep clean hands than it is to get dirty hands. Imagine playing in a sandlot, and you're trying to keep your hands clean. It would be impossible, and you'd easily get dirt everywhere. This wouldn't necessarily be the case if you were trying your best to keep them clean. Therefore, it's unfeasible to keep clean hands in this walk with Christ. However, we should still strive to have clean hands because, in that, we're seeking the heart and will of God.

Around roughly 2013, I had a dream, and it was specifically about clean hands. In the dream, I was at work, and I went into the bathroom stall, and as I was using the bathroom, I heard a loud trumpet sound. I then walked out calmly and went to the sink and began to wash my hands. There was a huge window in the bathroom, and as I was washing my hands, an extremely bright white light was shining into the bathroom. I looked at it and continued washing my hands. I then heard a voice, and it said, "Lead by example." I was thinking, *Lead by example*. Well, that's not that deep. However, the most meaningful things usually come from what we see as something simple or something small. The dream had me thinking of clean hands and leading by example by having clean hands. The scripture that then came to mind shortly after was Psalm 24:3–4, which said, "Who may ascend into the hill of the Lord? Who may stand in His holy place? He who has clean hands and a pure heart." I believe that

Psalm 24:3–4 aligned perfectly with the dream that I had in so many powerful ways.

Never become insecure because you don't have a "story." Your story is grace and mercy. It may not sound like everyone else's because it's yours! For those who don't have the cleanest story, there's nothing wrong with that either. We all have paths that have led us to this point right now in life. For we are His and He is ours. It doesn't matter how He became yours just that He did. The funny thing is that we have always been His, which is significant. We must become comfortable in our story and embrace that we have God now and not get too caught up in the how. Don't make things deeper than what it is. The point is we have God, and we need to build on that relationship and stand on that. A funny story is once my family and I took a vacation to Philadelphia when I was about seven or eight to go to Sesame Place. While we were there, I got pressured to get on this waterslide that I really didn't want to get on. As I got on and was going down the slide, I knew I was making a mistake. My journey to the end of the slide was rough, but for my sister, it was smoother. So when I got to the end of the slide, I panicked and went into the pool and went under. I remember going up and down, up and down. While I was going under, I could also hear my mother yelling from the top for someone to help me. I was clearly in panic mode. I then heard the lifeguard yelling, "Stand up!" as she was coming to help me. Yes, all I had to do was stand up.

I tell this story because it doesn't matter what you've done or how bad it seems to you. All you must do is stand up. The important thing is that you stand in the truth of who God is and believe that He sent His son to die on the cross for you. Your path doesn't matter as long as you decide to stand up. That should make you shout! Standing up is in comparison to standing on God and getting back to Him. It doesn't matter what you've done or what you've been through. Just stand up and get back to God. When you miss someone, you long to be in their presence, and you want to keep company with them. Do you keep company with God? Company is defined as the fact or condition of being with another person or others. It's basically an association, which means a direct link. Anyone connected to

God will receive well in their life because they are connected to the almighty, the all-knowing. However, when we disconnect ourselves from Him, we are then far from Him, and it can be hard for us to reach those things due to our lifestyle. We must stay connected to the almighty Father, not because you want the "benefits," but because He is God. We must start looking at things and situations with a "because He's God" attitude. Having this mindset is a good thing because even when you don't think He's looking out, He is. More so than that, even when we don't deserve Him, He's looking out for us. That indeed is the definition of a good God, a true Father.

My mother made this point very clear to me during my early college days. I don't really remember the specifics, but I had to follow some steps through the admissions process to be cleared to start classes. So last minute, I was scrambling to get things done, and it looked like I wasn't going to make the deadline. I ended up going up to the school the next day, which just so happened to be the day before classes started. Somehow someway, they did what they could to allow me to start classes on time. I can honestly say that I didn't deserve to be able to take classes because I made a dumb decision to wait until the last minute to go up there to get things done. They did everything that they could for me to be able to start classes, and I was grateful. I then went home and told my mom about what happened, and the first thing she said was "See, God be looking out for dumb people."

Initially, I started laughing, but shortly after, I fell to my knees with tears because God was indeed looking out for me. Even when we blatantly ignore what it is we're supposed to do or accidentally forget, God still looks out for us. To have a God that looks out for you despite the dumb decisions that we may make really shows you that we're truly *His. God looks out for us in ways we didn't even know was possible. Now imagine what He'd do for a righteous man. Psalm 37:25 states, "I have been young, and now I am old, yet have I not seen the righteous forsaken, nor his seed begging bread." This means that God is going to provide and take care of His; therefore, we must be *His. Yes, God still loves us and looks after us regardless. However, there's a difference when you have an understanding and you walk and operate out of being His. God will indeed look out for the righteous man. Therefore, if God can look out for people who are constantly doing wrong and making human mistakes, imagine what He'd do for the righteous. Therefore, I challenge you to strive to live a righteous lifestyle. This isn't something that's easy, but you must be willing. It must first start with the desire. You must long to be in that place. We are creatures who typically find ourselves where our hearts are. This means we must get to a point where our hearts long to be righteous, and in that, you will get there. It's simply amazing being *His and knowing that He'll never leave us or forsake us no matter how insignificant we may feel we are on the big scale of things. You are significant in His eyes.

John 10:14 reads, "I am the good shepherd, and I know My own and My own know Me." As a shepherd, He looks out for us and provides for us. Here's a great comparison. My mom brought a fish home. Mind you, we all were older, so no one was ardent about the fish. However, we agreed to feed it. The hard part was just remembering to do so. So it was probably three weeks after she bought it, and that was my first time noticing the fish again since it arrived. At the time, I'd like to think that I was a busy individual and had a lot on my plate; however, my mother was the one with a perpetual of things on her plate. This one instance, I remembered we had a fish, and I went to her in a frenzy and said, "I forgot we even had a fish. I haven't been feeding it."

My mom then calmly looked at me and said, "I feed him." It was mind-boggling because I knew everything that she had going on, yet she still remembered the insignificant fish in my eyes. She saw the importance of the fish. I was personally taken back by it because I knew how hectic the past few weeks had been, yet he was fed. I say this to say, God won't forget about you. Just like the fish, we may see ourselves as insignificant in God's eyes, but He sees us as *His. Regardless of the number of people in the world and the issues going on, He sees you as worthy. You won't be forgotten. For we are His and He is ours. The next time you think you're forgotten, know that you are so very important in God's eyes. That should make you smile. You are His. So even when you're missing God and you know you've strayed away, know that He sees you. Return to God.

Snakes in the Land

One night as I was sleeping, I had a dream. In my dream, I was with my family on what seemed like a camping sight. My mom, sister, and I went into what I'm assuming was the community cabin. Shortly after we entered, I walked out and was walking to a different location. As I was walking, I had my phone in my hand. I was consumed by it indeed. As I continued to walk, I kept my head down. I was comfortable. I then instantly heard a voice say, "Snakes in the land," but it was subtle. I took another step with my head still down. Then I heard the voice again loudly and rapidly, saying, "Snakes in the land, snakes in the land." I looked up instantly, and there was a huge python standing at about 15 feet tall with his mouth open, ready to devour me. If I would've taken one more step, there would've been no turning back.

At that very moment in the dream, I woke up. As I laid in my bed, all kinds of emotions were running through my head. What am I consumed by? Are my spiritual eyes open? Are snakes in my circle? What does the snake represent? Those all are questions I began to ask myself. Though I may not know precisely what the dream meant, I know I learned some fruitful lessons. Sometimes, we can be so consumed by our own intentions that we block out the voice of God when He's only trying to protect us from our own steps. We must put our own personal desires that typically consume our minds aside. Matthew 16:24 says, "Whoever wants to be my disciple must deny themselves and take up their cross and follow me." Therefore, we must do just that, follow Him. It then goes on in Matthew 16:25 and reads, "For whoever wants to save their life will lose it, but whoever loses their life for me will find it." This is simply stating that sometimes, we think we know the correct way when we don't. Proverbs 14:12 says it best, "There is a way that appears right but in the end, leads to death." That verse correlates directly to my dream. Sometimes, we get so consumed by what we "think" is right, but we're leading ourselves into a snake—death. Don't be deceived by what you think is right. Lean on God. In that, you'll be alert and able to realize when you're coming up on a snake. No one wants to willingly lead themselves astray. You must trust your instincts. If something is telling you, "Get out of there," or your intuitiveness says something's not right, you must listen to that.

Don't put yourself in a compromising situation because you were so caught up in the "moments" of life that you forget to pay attention to the warning signs. If you're in tune with the Holy Spirit, God will speak to you and give you signs before the snake appears in your face. However, we have to make sure we aren't consumed by the intriguing distractions to where we have drowned out the voice of God in our lives. Never allow your voice to be louder than God's.

Know Yourself

When I was off at college in Lakeland, Florida, we decided to go with a friend to Orlando to a church. Originally, I thought it was going to be a youth event. It wasn't. The fact that it wasn't a youth event wasn't a big deal because it was still church! So while we were heading there, we began to get lost. At that moment, I started getting this unsettled feeling in my gut. Plus, no one had been to this church before. When we finally did pull up, we were extremely late. My heart was beating mightily fast. It's safe to say I was afraid. It was I and three others, and as we began to get out, I was moving stiffly and slowly. They asked me what was wrong, and all I could do was shake my head. We began to walk in, and I was second to last entering in. As we were walking down this hallway to enter the church building, my heart was pounding, and everything was telling me no. Then suddenly, I stopped walking and was planted, and I literally couldn't move. They asked what was wrong, and all I could say was, "No, no, no." I knew what I knew, and I didn't need anyone else to cosign or to feel what I felt. My sister and I sat in the car during the entire service. Yes, we sat in the car for over an hour in half in not the best neighborhood. Nothing "bad" occurred in the service from my understanding. However, it was a deliverance service, and I knew my fears and what I was struggling with.

My entire childhood and part of my young adult life, I've dealt with the spirit of fear. At that point in my life, I had made huge strides when it pertained to certain things, and I knew that going in would just set me back. Therefore, you must know yourself and stick to what you know is best for you. Everyone won't agree with you, and everyone won't understand. Through all of it, you are the one who will have to live with the consequences of your decisions.

So it's okay if you're not ready for something—know yourself and know what could set you back. Everyone's different, but it's our job to know ourselves. As I look back on that time in my life, I'm proud of myself. I was extremely courageous to make my "no means no," as my mother would say. I knew myself, and I knew not a single person in sight could feel what I felt. Therefore, I wasn't persuaded. You have to know what makes you feel unsettled and what your spirit man doesn't agree with. I'm by no means saying walk in fear and run from things that make you uncomfortable. I am saying know yourself so well that you know when something just isn't right and when your spirit man doesn't agree.

As life goes on and your walk with God continues to grow and you maneuver through your walk with God, you'll need to know what agrees and aligns with your spirit man and what doesn't—in more practical terms, what agrees with Christ who lives inside of you and what doesn't. It's okay if you're standing alone in the flesh. However, feel secure that in the spirit, you are not alone. Know that there is agreement. Always strive to be on one accord with God and not man.

Our Father Knows What We Need

One day, I was sitting in the car during my break, and I had a missed call. I then went to my call history, and I realized that I called on this particular person all the time. They were who I called on the most—just as you can look in your phone and see the history of who you've called on. What if there was a way to see who we call upon in the crisis, tragedy, and even times of rejoicing. The reason why it's important to use the parallel of who we talk to on our cell phones is that that shows relationships. We call on our friends and loved ones regardless of what's going on, good or bad. This is because we have an established relationship with these people. Do you have an established relationship with God? If you don't have an established relationship with Him, you must build one.

Up to this point, I've told multiple stories just to say the same thing—which is simply, build a relationship with God. It's a must. It's vital to our lives. We must look to Him. Have you ever called someone when you needed them to give you something, whether it was some advice, comfort, or just simply their time to listen, and you didn't receive what you reached out for? Well, when you call on God, He gives us exactly what we need. Sometimes, it may not seem like it at that moment, but He's all-knowing—omniscient. God knows our spoken and unspoken needs.

One evening, my need was so inordinate. I didn't have to speak my need, but it was as if it was projected loud on an intercom. I was struggling financially, and my parents knew that. So we were all in a hotel because we were heading to Maryland. I don't remember exactly how the conversation began, but I knew we were talking about money. One thing led to the next, and then my father was like, "Let's play a game." He said, "Who's in?" and without even knowing the game, I agreed. I mean, after all, it was a game, and games are meant to be fun. My father said to us, "How much money do you have on you?" I was thinking, *Aren't we supposed to be playing a game?* My father then said, "Don't say the amount out loud. Just look." The next part was the key to it all. He then said, "If you're playing, the game is whoever has the most money on them takes all. Do you trust what's in your hand? If not, just say I'm out." When my dad said that, everyone pulled out but my father and me. I was extremely nervous because, I mean, after all, he's my father, and I know he has more money than me. However, the game wasn't who had the most money overall. It was who physically had the most money on them. Let's just say I had over $300 in cash on me, and that was because I needed that money for a photo shoot that we had coming up in Maryland. Even though I was nervous, I had to trust what was in my hand.

Then the moment came, we had to reveal what we had. I went first, and I had about $300 to show for. I wasn't extremely confident, but I already made a bold decision by agreeing to play. Therefore, I had to stand by my decision, knowing that I could potentially lose it all. My dad showed his hand, and he had about $200 on him. However, little did I know, he had just given my mom some of their money to put in her wallet because it's bigger than his wallet. So let's just say if he didn't do that, I wouldn't have had a shot at winning the game. He knew that, and I'd like to believe he knew the amount I had on me as well. The reason for that is, shortly before getting to the hotel, we stopped at the bank, and he knew how much we had to pay the photographer. He knew what I had, and he knew my need. That's exactly how God is. God will bless you when you least expect it. But do you have faith? By no means am I saying risk what you have in the possibility of getting more. That was my dad, and somewhere inside, he knew my need, and I didn't have to say a word. I trusted my father.

Do you trust your heavenly Father? Do you trust He sees and knows your need? Do you trust that He will move accordingly to

His timing? I had that very same need weeks ago, but God knew what He was doing in that hotel that night. Not only did I need a financial breakthrough, but also I needed to be uplifted and encouraged. God provided all that in one and in the perfect timing. God is indeed omniscient, and we need to heed always. The crazy thing is God knows what we need versus what we want. We can't fool God. Therefore, we can be waiting for God to do something that we've tried to convince ourselves that it's a need when God knows that it's not. He will move when it's time. We can't move God. He moves in His perfect timing. This is all a part of being His. For I am His and He is mine. Therefore, we give up our personal desires, and we submit 100 percent to God's plans. For you to do that, you must trust God. If you're bucking against God in every way, you may unknowingly doubt God. And if that's the case, you need to remind yourself of what He's done.

As our mom would say, "Check your faith file." James 1:2–8 speaks about faith and doubt. It reads, "My brethren, count it all joy when ye fall into divers temptations; knowing this, that the trying of your faith worketh patience. But let patience have her perfect work, that ye may be perfect and entire, wanting nothing. If any of you lack wisdom, let him ask of God, that giveth to all men liberally, and upbraideth not; and it shall be given him. But let him ask in faith, nothing wavering. For he that wavereth is like a wave of the sea driven with the wind and tossed. For let not that man think that he shall receive anything of the Lord. A double-minded man is unstable in all his ways." In simple terms, this is stated that you can't be of faith and of doubt because if so, you are double-minded and don't understand faith.

Where Your Gift Will Take You

Growing up, my family spent most of my childhood years in Maryland. During that time, we attended the same church. Therefore, many of the members became like family to us. So when we moved away, my parents kept in touch with a lot of the members. This one winter, in early 2017, we took a trip back to Maryland. We were all extremely excited, and we made plenty of rounds. In those rounds, we had to make sure to stop by some leader's house so they could see everyone. As kids, when we visited their house, my sister and I would always sit in the living room on the couch. On the other hand, our Parents and the leaders would all be at the dinner table. During this last visit, we were twenty-three and twenty-two, and we were heading to the couch like normal. Then randomly, the bishop stopped us and told us to have a seat at the table. We looked around in awe because he wanted us to have a seat at the table in the presence of greatness and wisdom. We were definitely shaken because we weren't expecting that at all. However, we knew our gifts allowed us to sit in that company even if maturity wise, we were in two different tiers.

That opportunity was definitely a propelling experience. Even though it allowed us to believe in ourselves and in our gifts, it also humbled us into knowing we had a lot to learn. We spent most of our time looking extremely interested and nodding our heads to all the good things that were said. And at one point while sitting there nodding my head, I thought of Proverbs 18:16. It reads, "A man's gift will make room for him, and bring him before great men." You must allow your gift to make room for you. However, you must be mature enough to know that it doesn't end there. What's a talent if you don't work on your craft? A waste of potential, right? Fight to be all you can be and offer your gift back to God. In this, you must also understand that the gifts God gave you call for you to prepare as well. Think about this, if you're in the NBA, you won't just show up to the game having been to no practices or shootarounds and then jump into the game. You just wouldn't do that regardless of Allen Iverson's beliefs. You'd put the time and effort into your gift so that you can truly offer your best. However, that doesn't mean if you had no preparation that suddenly, your gift would disappear. But it does mean you'd be cutting yourself short and lowering your ceiling drastically.

Preparation allows you to maximize your gift to its fullest capacity. In a way, it's you offering something back to your gift. Oprah says it best, "Luck is preparation meeting the moment of opportunity." I love that because it's true. Preparation prepares you for the good that'll come your way. It's telling God thank you and enhancing what He's placed in your hand. It's nice when things work out even when you don't prepare. But what about the times it doesn't? What about the times you walk away, knowing you could have given more? Don't allow your unwillingness to prepare to hinder your strives toward excellence. You are better than that. Don't create bad muscle memory. We can all be better. We can all offer a little bit more. But are you allowing your gift to take you places, or are you sitting on what God's given you? Your gift can make room for you, but you can unknowingly leave the room.

So when I say, "Are you sitting on what God's given you, I mean just that?" Most of my life, I've dealt with the fear of the unknown. I didn't want to go to new places alone, meet new people, start a new job, or anything that made me feel uncomfortable even if it was for the betterment of my situation. I would turn down promotions that required some sort of newness or dumb myself down so I wouldn't get picked for these things—sitting on what God gave me. Your gift can make room for you, but will you fill it? You have to tell yourself, "I'm coming for everything my insecurities said I couldn't have." You have to allow your gift to make room for you and not allow fear or anything to take that from you. Your gift was created for you, and you were created for your gift. I had to walk out these words when I first got married and moved to Jacksonville. My gift made room for me, but I was struggling to fill the room. I shrunk myself when indeed, it was time to grow and occupy the space that God put me in. So yes, your gift will make room for you, but make sure you know how to fill the room.

Get It for Yourself

There comes a point in your life where you have to do things on your own. The way you used to amble around life just isn't cutting it. You have to advance. Jeremiah 1:5 says, "I knew you before I formed you in your mother's womb. Before you were born, I set you apart and appointed you as my prophet to the nations." Do you still know God? It's so easy to get caught up in the hustle and bustle of life. But we must unsnarl ourselves and begin to know God. There was a point in my life where I missed God and knew I missed God. Yet there wasn't much that I knew at the time. Therefore, I was left searching for something I didn't find for three years. Though I was still a kid, I felt like the table was always set for me to eat at one point in my life.

Now let me explain what I mean. When I went to the church prior, God's presence was there. The word was good, and I was learning and "eating." Yet I never fixed my own plate. By the time I'd show up, someone's already made the food, made my plate, and all I had to do was sit and eat. God's presence was set. That was just the season that I was in. I was incapable of doing much but eating. The struggle I'm speaking of came when we couldn't find a church home in California. We looked and looked, but nothing was home. Therefore, I was in a foreign area, and I was looking for food. I missed God. But what I didn't know was that I was His, and He was mine. So in actuality, it didn't matter where I went. I could experience God anywhere. I didn't have to be in my favorite church. Yet, at that time, I was amateurish and didn't understand the lesson in my trials.

Now as I look back, those three years were vital in my relationship with God because my faith was tested. I had to learn how to fix my own plate. I had to learn how to pray, worship, and read my word. I was spending more time in the kitchen. Through this, I then appreciated the table more. When someone was anointed, I could feel it. When God's presence was strong, I soaked it up. When the food was given, I ate all of it. I learned to appreciate His anointed and the house of God. I was adding to the kingdom and not just taking it. Though this wasn't the easiest thing in my life, it was vital to my tomorrow. The moral to most of the stories is to "trust the process." As a society, I think we've begun to fall more and more in love with the end result that we've forgotten there's even a process, to begin with. The times of not being able to "eat" allowed me to see that there was even a process, to begin with. Prior, I would only see the end result because that's all I was conditioned to see. Food was given to me, so I always wanted to start eating when I felt "hungry." When I couldn't eat, I missed eating. I'd do anything to be at the table again.

My question to you is, Will you do anything to be with God again? We've become conditioned to this world, and at times, we can be fooled to believe that feeling distant from God is normal. However, consider this, you are the dictator of what becomes the standard in your life. Do you want God distant or not? That's something you'll have to ask yourself. We can't compare our lives and how we live in the world. If you do, you'll begin to get satisfied and thinking you're "ahead." Don't be the one in the race that has a slight lead but loses it because you keep looking behind you.

One day, I was working at a supermarket, and we had to mop the entire store. It was just myself and one other person who was mopping the large store. For whatever reason, that day, I wasn't having the best of days. I was upset because I felt like I was doing so much "good" things in life, as trying to live right. However, I felt like I wasn't seeing the results of that. My life felt the same as others who were living in any kind of way. I felt it was unfair, and there wasn't much separation. I was moping as all this was running through my mind. At that moment, I then felt convicted because I was missing the bigger picture. It's our job as humans who were created by God to serve God. So just because some choose not to serve God doesn't mean I'm perfect, and only good will come my way just because I've decided to live right. On the bigger scale of things, I've only done a portion of what's actually required of me. I still fall short daily, and I am still ridding myself of ungodly things. So no, we're no better than the rest. However, I thank God that I'm actually in the race.

So remember, we don't compare ourselves to the world and non-believers. We compare our lives to the word and according to God's purpose for our lives. For I am His and He is mine. Sometimes, we may feel like we "miss" God, but that's really not the case. When operating out of the flesh, it can be hard to put into words what our spirit man is really going through. As humans, we usually can only define it as "missing" when it's actually a step deeper. It's more like a yearning to get closer to God, almost like a demand for more. We have to understand when it's time to go to the next dimension in God that "breast milk" no longer sustains the body. The body, at some point, requires table food to take the body where it needs to go. It can't go to its next phase in life, intaking the same thing that was designed for its previous state of demand.

Are you holding yourself back? Don't become comfortable with breast milk. It's a temporary feeding phase to get you to where you need to be in order to step into your next. Your spirit man is yearning table food. It has outgrown the things that used to sustain it. Therefore, there's a void that is probably unexplainable. When I was a child, I used to call all worship songs "slow songs." This one particular slow song, "Thirst for You" by CeCe Winans, is a perfect melody for the yearning I'm speaking of. Our soul quenches to be filled in this dry and barren land. We have to be intentional in doing all we can to make sure we're constantly growing in Christ. Otherwise, we can easily teach and sway ourselves to become content and begin to live a complacent life. We want to stay away from this. It's a trick from the enemy. When we feel ourselves slipping and it's becoming difficult to grow your relationship with God, that's when you have to press in the most.

While I was off at school at Southeastern University, I had to learn to press in and pull on the anointing. During the times when you don't feel God is usually when you need to press in the most. I would go to chapel some days and would leave without a touch. Then I made a decision that I wasn't going to continuously go to the chapel and leave the same. I'd go to the chapel and block everything and everyone out because I was simply there to get mine. I desired

God's presence. If you have no desire to be in God's presence here on earth, why do you desire heaven? Desire is defined as a strong feeling of wanting to have something or wishing for something to happen. It's a want, aspiration, inclination, impulse, yearning, longing, craving, hankering, eagerness, or determination. I think it's easy to say that if you desire God, you'll do all you can to grow in Him.

Matthew 7:7 says, "Ask and it will be given to you; seek and you will find; knock and the door will be opened to you." Matthew 7:7 shows that if you really desire God, he'll be sure to meet you. For I am His and He is mine. It's time to get yours. We must press through the crowd and touch the hem of His garment. How bad do you want God? When you're really fed up with the way you've been living life, when you're really tired of your dry season, you'll make a change.

Now let's talk about practical life adjustments to get closer to God. If getting closer to God is the goal, you have to have a game plan of things you'll put in place to ensure that result. You have to ask yourself, "What's a part of my daily routine that's enhancing my walk with God?" If you were in a relationship, there would be intentional things you'd implement into your day to keep your relationship going—whether that's a text, lunch date, movies, phone call, or simple daily tasks together. You would do things to keep the relationship going and growing. We have to do the same with God. Here are some simple tasks I do to help grow my relationship with God:

- Listen to Christian music.
- Listen to YouTube sermons in my car heading to work or podcasts.
- Read scriptures before bed.
- Read Christian books.
- Talk with Christian friends about God.
- Read Christian blogs.
- Display Christian behavior (being kind, considerate, loving, etc.).

Now you don't have to do these exact things, but you must do something. Growing up, our parents would always tell us the saying "If you fail to plan, you plan to fail." You don't want to fail to get closer to God. So take the pressure off yourself and begin to implement some simple yet effective adjustments. Make it a priority of yours. Usually, when you make something a priority, you have to cast something aside. I think we all can easily agree to the idea of making God a priority. But are we willing to cast things aside that's been a priority to allow God in? That could mean something or someone you love, something familiar or comfortable, or something you're attached to.

A great parallel to this is growing up and learning to save. As a kid, it's hard to understand the aspect of saving. However, our parents would always tell us when we got money on different occasions that saving was an option. Of course, as a kid, I wanted to spend my five dollars at the dollar tree on candy and chips. I didn't want to give up that chance. However, I didn't understand that choosing not to spend the money on candy and saving wasn't a loss. That it actually was a gain. By me not spending the money, I would've been able to save for a bigger reward. I could've saved and purchased a huge dollhouse. You deciding to discipline yourself and set boundaries or guardrails in your life is setting you up for your dollhouse—a stronger relationship with God. So don't get upset because you can't buy chips or toys at the dollar tree store. It will be worth it in the end when the reward is great.

Adjustment is defined as a small alteration or movement made to achieve a desired fit, appearance, or result. In the bigger picture, the things you'd cast aside is minor compared to your relationship with God. For I am His and He is mine. Many of us have grown up in the church, or at some point, our lives were reintroduced to God. You've probably strayed away at some point in your life and realized that you need to get back to Him. One morning, I was heading to work, and I was in a rush. That particular morning, I didn't have time for extracurricular activities, especially not a spider. So as I was getting in my car, I noticed a spider on the outside mirror. It was huge. I rushed into the car to ensure it wouldn't touch me. After I jumped in the car, I slammed the door, and when I did that, the spider began to move farther away from the mirror. He had a long spiderweb going who knows where.

So as I began to drive, I kept looking at him. He began to crawl farther and farther away from the mirror. I was set on him falling off if I drove faster, but I was in for a rude awakening. As I got on the highway, it began to rain. I was determined that I was going to put him through some "stuff" so that he wouldn't survive. At this point, I had already been driving for almost ten minutes, and he was still hanging on. Just when I thought he was going to fall off, he did something so simple, yet it blew my mind. He began to crawl back to the mirror and went and hid in the cracks of where he had traveled so far from. I was so upset because I was trying to get rid of him. Then I thought about what I really just witnessed, and I was in awe of God once again.

Sometimes, we have to do like the spider and, in the midst of storms, get back to safety. The enemy may try to throw all he can and then some to break you. Don't forget the safety behind the mirror. Run to God. Isaiah 25:4 reads, "You have been a refuge for the poor, a refuge for the needy in their distress, a shelter and a shade from the heat. For the breath of the ruthless is like a storm driving against a wall." The spider held on during the storm and did everything it could to get back to its safety. Are you going to continue to fight the trials alone, or are you going to surrender it all to God in order to get to that next level in Him?

God has to become our go-to in all things. Therefore, you have to train your mind *now* to think in ways it might've never thought. However, the reward will be great. The reward is God. It's just like athletes. That basketball player in March is only going to be able to perform in the tournament off the training that they went through throughout the year. Players don't just show up during March Madness without the work of the season. You'll never see a player do something they've never done in practice. We must create muscle memory. Muscle memory is defined as the ability to reproduce a particular movement without conscious thought, acquired as a result of frequent repetition of that movement. So is God your go-to? In order for us to continue to go higher in Him, He must become our go-to. We must have that mentality that we're going to get it for ourselves, and we aren't waiting for a particular moment. Your moment is now.

Don't Believe the Lies

John 8:44 is such an important verse because it's Jesus explaining the devil's true character. As Christians, we must understand who speaks the truth and who doesn't. John 8:44 reads, "You are of your father, the devil, and it is your will to practice the desires [which are characteristic] of your father. He was a murderer from the beginning and does not stand in the truth because there is no truth in him. When he lies, he speaks what is natural to him, for he is a liar and the father of lies and half truths." We have to have discernment and ignite our spiritual eyes and ears. The devil isn't going to feed you with random lies because he knows you're smarter than that. He'll come with half truths or play off your insecurities. If you don't know the truth, you'll believe the lies.

For years and years, the devil had been trying to torment me in my sleep. The tactic he used was to try to make me feel powerless through dreams and other belittling tactics. The lies worked simply because I didn't know the truth. I didn't know I had power. A breakthrough moment for me was when I was invited to an invitational retreat. It changed everything. On the first day of the retreat, I noticed I didn't have a particular bag of mine that I packed. In that bag was my belt that I wore every day. We parked our cars at the bottom of the hill because they didn't want any vehicles on the property. Therefore, it was a long way to walk. So for a few days, I went without my belt, knowing I needed it. So this one particular morning, while on the retreat, I woke up adamant about going to go get my belt. By this point, everyone in the house knew about my belt being left in the car because I kept mentioning it. I stood at the door and explained to my mom, apostle, and my sister why I was going to go get it regardless of the weather.

So I covered up and went outside with my sister to go get my belt. On the way down the hill, the wind was strong, and I was questioning my decision. However, once I made it to the car and grabbed my belt, everything I went through to get it was worth it. Later on, during a session, the apostle saw me with my belt on, and she smiled and said, "You were getting that belt regardless, huh?" I laughed and nodded my head. During that session, she just so happened to be talking about putting on the armor of God. As she was going through the armor of God, she stopped on the belt of truth and used me as an example. She explained how you have to be determined to get the belt of truth. I didn't care about anything else but to get my belt! Are you determined to get the truth? The enemy will try to do whatever he can to get you to buy in to his lies and deception. But you must remember what's around your waist—the belt of truth (Ephesians 6:10–20). So when you put your belt on in the mornings, be reminded of the truth and know what God and God's word says about you. Therefore, resist the devil and the devil's lies.

James 4:7 says, "Submit yourselves then to God. Resist the devil, and he will flee from you." Resist is defined as "withstand the action or effect of." It's to combat, weather, endure, or to oppose something. Therefore, we have to stop allowing, accepting, aiding, assisting, or helping the devil wreak havoc in our lives by not resisting and raising up a standard against the devil. Isaiah 59:19 reads, "So shall they fear the rising of the son. When the enemy shall come in like a flood, the Spirit of the Lord shall lift up a standard against him." This goes back to James 4:7 that we have to submit ourselves to God, and in that, we resist the devil. Through God, we can resist the devil. We can't fight this battle alone. A way to practically resist the devil is keeping yourself sharp in the word and continuing to build and lean on your relationship with God. Also, remembering to keep people around you who are walking this walk and resisting the devil as well. It's always easier when you're going through something difficult to go through it with someone else. It makes the load seem a little lighter. I say it like this: "Rest and immerse under what's to come, give and cultivate what's behind, and illuminate and elevate with those you stand." All three levels of this quote are extremely important when dealing with temptation and life and just life in general.

- Rest and immerse under what's to come.
  - o You position yourself under those who've been where you're going.
  - o You have someone feeding into you or guiding you and warning you along the way.

- Give and cultivate what's behind.
  - o Share your temptations and how you've overcome some things to those coming behind you to prevent someone else from falling in the devil's familiar traps.

- Illuminate and elevate with those we stand.
  - o This one is critical because sometimes, you just need to know you're not alone in this thing.
  - o You surround yourself with people who are trying to defeat the enemy and not cosigning with him.
  - o We were created to be the light of the world.

These three principles are a way of life that I believe recent generations have strayed away from. It's simply discipleship. We have to get back to discipline. In order to do that, we have to get back to being able to be disciplined. Therefore, accept discipleship and don't allow the devil to distract you with temptations. That's all temptation is—a distraction from what you should be focused on. We have to look at it like we have somewhere to go, and we can't be held up in getting to our destination. I remember this one particular evening. I was leaving work and got on the highway like normal to head home. As soon as I got on the highway, I noticed some stoppage less than a mile down the road. I immediately felt like there was another way that I could go. I was then tempted to take the next exit and go the back way because that's what everyone else was doing. So at that moment, that's exactly what I did—even though my GPS was saying otherwise. My GPS was actually telling me to stay on the highway and not get off. As soon as I got off, my GPS was trying to reroute me once again back to the highway. As I continued to head the back way, my GPS added approximately twenty minutes to my time. I was irked.

At this point, I was sure my GPS was wrong because I didn't see anything on the road that would add twenty minutes. Then it happened. I turned down a road, and I could see cars backed up in a line for miles. I then heeded what my GPS was saying, and I turned around. At this point, I was following my GPS because I thought it was taking me a new way home. Then I noticed that it was actually taking me back to the highway! As I was heading to get onto the highway, I looked to the left and could see the same stoppage that I was stuck in. Being flustered is an understatement. But little did I know, as soon as I got back on the highway, traffic was smooth sailing again. No one was really on the road. Prior, I couldn't see that far down the road because the overpass was blocking the road ahead. Therefore, if I was just patient and resisted the temptation to follow everyone else and listened to my GPS (God), I wouldn't have wasted so much time.

Don't fall into the distractions of the enemy. It's just a temptation to get you off, of course, of where you're supposed to be. We have to make sure we continue to build a strong relationship with God and surround ourselves with people who are going to help guide us down the lighted path. You have to first identify the temptations in your life in order to be better prepared. The devil is a liar, and we have to be equipped in order for us not to fall in his deceitful traps. So don't be pusillanimous. We must be strong and of good courage (Joshua 1:9). What's the truth? Proverbs 3:5–6 says, "Trust in the Lord with all your heart and lean not on your own understanding; in all your ways submit to him, and he will make your paths straight."

Push

Everything that's been said in this book so far won't mean anything without a push. We have to wake up every day with intentions to push past everything to get to what we want. God is the goal, and God is infinite. Therefore, our yen for Him shall be forever prevalent. Now you may be asking yourself, "How do I *push?*"

The *P* is for purposeful planning. We must plan according to our purpose and the purpose God has for our lives. This indeed is what will launch us into our next and point us down the guided path. For man makes plans, but the Lord ordains steps (Proverbs 16:9). Purposeful is defined as "having or showing determination or resolve." Therefore, it's intentional—which brings me to Habakkuk 2:2, "Write down the vision and make it plain." This means we have to first see it and then believe it and then plan for it. I think we've all had matters in our life where we wanted to do something, whether it was to start a mom-and-pop shop or to become a lawyer. We've all had aspirations that subsequently failed to come to past in our lives. This is because we usually get stuck after the "see it" phase in our *push*. This, however, can be a good thing at times, for this is what points us in the proper direction for our lives.

The "believe it" phase is the momentum behind the vision. Believing is what can catapult you into making plans. So if you fail to believe, you'll never plan. Believe, according to Merriam-Webster, is defined as to accept (something) as true, feel sure of the truth. Have you accepted what God says about you as truth? Now you may be asking yourself what God says about me. Well, I'm glad you asked. Psalm 8:5 says, "You have made him a little lower than the heavenly beings and crowned him with glory and honor." This means we were created in the spiritual likeness of God. Glory was also placed on our heads, and we're wrapped in honor. We are a royal priesthood (1 Peter 2:9). He also knows the plans He has for us (Jeremiah 29:11). Therefore, the purposeful planning will come with getting to know God and seeking His face. So we first have to see it and then believe it and then plan for it in that order to ensure you're purposefully planning in your life. Make God's word true in your heart and start planning according to your purpose.

The next thing in your *push* is the *U*. The *U* is for unique umbrella. I'm a believer in getting to the root definition if you can't tell already. With that said, umbrella is defined as a protecting force or influence. In this context, it's a representation of your covering. This concept is juxtaposed with the fences analogy in a previous chapter. Growing up, our parents would always say things like, "That's outside of the covering," or "That's outside of the umbrella." As a kid, I didn't really understand, but I absolutely understand the importance now. We must live with a covering in our lives. It's vital. Psalm 91:3 says, "He rescues you from the snare of fowler hoping to destroy you: He covers you with His feathers, and you find shelter underneath His." Therefore, you have to have a covering to get to where you're trying to get to in Him. God is our umbrella. His feathers are what will protect us and will provide shelter.

Through this journey, we also need spiritual mentors to help get us through the turbulence of life. So as you take up your cross daily and yearly, it's vital that you have a covering, meaning people in your life who will cover you in prayer spiritually—as in discipleship or mentors. Sometimes, life can get tough, and you just need to know that there's someone else out there who wants you to be all you're called to be in God and is constantly interceding on your behalf—someone who has simply walked down the same path you're on and will pray you through. The unique umbrella is important because it's tailored to who you are and who God's called you to be.

The saying "It takes a village to raise a child" used to bother me in previous years. The reason for this annoyance pertaining to this saying was particularly because my "village" looked different from most. I subconsciously wanted my village to look like everyone else's around me. Yet God had a unique plan for His unique child. You are

God's unique son/daughter. Therefore, He's sent a unique village. Your village may be your grandmother, uncle, sister, and neighbor— as other persons may be their mother, father, cousin, and friend. God sends the village for the child. He knows you. He will send what you need to you in His timing. A lot of times, we miss what God's sending our way because we expect it to look a certain way. Yet God sends it the way He sees fit. God is unmoved by our personal inclination. God sends what He feels you need in your season when He sees fit for it to be delivered. He may not come when you want Him, but He's always on time as the old saints would say.

The S in your *push* is crucial. The S stands for "stamping your season." Now you know I have to give a definition for stamping. One can define stamping as "to identify, characterize, or reveal." Check this out! A postage stamps purpose is evidence of payment of the postage. That is something to shout hallelujah about, and let me tell you why. When you stamp your season, it's evidence that the season is over. The payment was sent when Jesus Christ hung on the cross for us. Through that, we are overcomers. When you stamp your season, you're declaring it over and sending it off just like a postage stamp. You're professing that you went through something, but it no longer has a hold on you. The reason this is crucial to your growth is that we're going to go through some "stuff" in our lives. However, you'll overcome, and you'll need reminding of that through those valley low places.

Remember what God carried you through. Remember that He's the God that you can place your burdens in the "shopping cart." Don't forget what He brought you through. Be reminded in your low season of how He picked you up, turned you around, and placed your feet on solid ground. He was God then, and He's still God now. Speak those things that God allowed you to triumph over back to the devil in your dry season. I dare you. See yourself victorious when you feel defeated. Dig deep in your down season and push to that next level of anointing. Shout in your low season and show God what you're made of.

One year during the flu season, my sister caught type A and type B flu. Just a couple of days later, I started to not feel well. I went to the doctor, and sure enough, I had the flu as well, type A and B. Obviously, having the flu alone was terrible, but having type A and B was devastating. Not to add, our parents were out of town. A few days had gone by, and we were struggling. If you've ever had the flu, you know the draining and helpless feeling that you feel. The only bright side was that we were at least in it together. On about day three of the flu, I had had enough. I reminded myself of who I was. I'm a daughter of a true king. I've witnessed healing and miracles before. The Bible said we are to do greater works than Christ. The reason we don't see this manifested entirely is that we have little faith.

At that moment, I shook myself and reminded myself of who God is and what He's done for me. I cut on my worship music, and despite the fact that I had absolutely no energy, my head was banging, and that I could barely stand, I worshiped Him. I showed God that even when I'm at my worst, I can, and I will *push* through. I walked around that house, speaking in tongues and commanding my body to heal. This is why you stamp your season. It reminds and encourages you when you're weak that He is strong. That when you're sick, He's healed before. So remember when you want to give up that He's rescued you before. Stamping your season is reminding you that Christ has already paid the cost. Understanding this in your *push* is pivotal in walking out being completely *His. For I am His and He is mine. I pray this helps you. I pray this falls on good ground. Lord, help us.

Lastly, in your *push*, there's the *H*. The *H* stands for "humbly *His." Throughout the entire book, we've been learning what it means to be *His. So let's focus on "humbly." Humble is defined as "having or showing a modest or low estimate of one's own importance." The key to that is one's *own* importance. There's nothing wrong with believing that you have some significant importance to something. But we have to know that this walk, this denying of flesh and being, *His is about Him. We are to be meek. Matthew 5:5 reads, "Blessed are the meek, for they will inherit the earth." There is a return for the humbled. We must learn that through our meekness, we are strong. We all want to be lifted by God, but we're missing the humility. James 4:10 reads, "Humble yourself before the Lord, and he will lift you up." The elevation doesn't humble you. It's the humbling that elevates you. James 4:7–9, the verse before, says, "Submit yourself, then, to God. Resist the devil, and he will flee from you. Come near to God, and he will draw near to you. Wash your hands, you sinners, and purify your hearts, you double-minded. Grieve, mourn, and wail. Change your laughter to mourning and your joy to gloom."

This book is called *His for a reason. For I am His and He is mine. James 4:7–9 explains the dynamic of our relationship with God at times. The message version makes it very clear. "You're cheating on God. If all you want is your own way, flirting with the world every chance you get, you end up enemies of God and his ways. And do you suppose God doesn't care? The proverb has it that He's a fiercely jealous lover. And what he gives in love is for better than anything else you'll find. It's common knowledge that God goes against willful pride. God gives grace to the willing humble. So let God work His will in you. Tell a loud no to the devil and watch him scamper. Say a quiet yes to God, and he'll be there in no time. Quit dabbling in sin. Purify your inner life. Quit playing the field. Hit bottom, and cry your eyes out. The fun and games are over. Get serious, really serious. Get down on your knees before the Master. It's the only way you'll get on your feet."

It's time to humble ourselves and fall to our knees. It's time we stop flirting with the world and commit ourselves fully to God. We are *His, so stop waiting for the perfect time to commit. He's waiting for you. *His arms are open. Humble yourself. Become *His because He is ours. We were created for Him. Take a minute and think about that. Think about all the things and people we put above Him. We were shaped and created for His glory. We have to humble ourselves under our Father again. One of my favorite scriptures that ties in directly is 1 Peter 5:6–7. It reads, "Humble yourself, then, under God's mighty hand. So that He will lift you up in His own good time. Leave all your worries with Him because He cares for you."

This verse is easier read than done. I remember a time in my life when I wanted particular things to happen for me—whether that was a certain job, promotion, speaking opportunities, relationships, this book, or just anything I didn't currently possess. I would doubt myself and ultimately get frustrated with God. But what I didn't understand was that humbling myself is needed before the elevation. Humbling myself is what would allow me to sustain the weight with the height. By humbling yourself under God and His timing, it's showing God that you trust Him. It's training you to understand that the weight is in God's hands. All you have to do is hold the position. You have to be determined to push through everything to see God manifest in your life.

On this day, today, as I'm writing this, I went to a fast-food restaurant. I had previously visited this restaurant the day before and didn't have a so pleasant experience. I found the worst thing you can find—hair in your food! I was upset yesterday, but that was yesterday's problems. Therefore, I intentionally went back to the same restaurant for my lunch the next day. I'm a quite idiosyncratic individual. So as I pull through the driveway, I was determined to have a better experience. I trusted the franchise enough to know there's no way that I won't have a better experience. There's a reason they continue to hold the position of respect in so many fast-food goers' minds. I tested them.

As I pulled up to the window, I was eager to see how this would unravel. He handed me my food with the biggest smile ever and said, "Have a good day." I proceeded to hand him my card, and he said, "It's already paid for." I had a bewilderment look on my face, and he smiled and ensured that it was paid for. I drove off, and, of course, I cried! I cried because it's the same for God. It's already paid for. By Him sending His only begotten Son Jesus Christ to die on the cross for our sins, that gives us access to Him. We have access to God because it's paid for. We just have to humble ourselves and go back to Him. We have to humble ourselves and realize that we can't do this thing alone. We need God to lift us up. Without God, we can't hold the weight. We have to humble ourselves under God and have complete faith—faith of a mustard seed, faith that can move mountains, faith that can make us whole. We have to have earthshaking faith. However, you can't have that kind of faith in God and His word until you completely humble yourself under Him.

A different afternoon as I was driving home from work, I was listening to music and worshipping. I had a vision of me reading the Book of Acts and being filled with the Holy Ghost. Now years prior, when I was about six years old, our parents came into our room one evening and asked us do we want to be filled with the Holy Ghost. Now take a minute and think about that. I was six years old! That just tells you the type of God-fearing parents I had and Christ-centered childhood I was blessed to have. But they came in that evening and asked, and I replied with a silent no and shook my head fast. Valencia, being the trailblazer and earthshaker that she was, said yes. She was seven. I sat on my bed and watched her be filled with the Holy Spirit and speak in tongues at the age of seven. For years after, I shied away from speaking in tongues because I believed I missed my moment. I knew I was filled with the Holy Spirit, but I was ready to see the evidence. I had enough faith in God and in His word to believe it could happen. However, after that vision, I thought nothing of it and went home and continued life as usual.

A few weeks later, I was in my room, worshiping. The song "Spirit Break Out" by Kim Walker began to play. As the song played, I grabbed my Bible, not even thinking about the previous vision. I had decided at that moment, I was going to experience what they originally experienced in the upper room. I turned to Acts 2, and before I began to read, I prayed. I prayed that God would fill me with the Holy Spirit and for His word to manifest in me. I began to read Acts 2:1–4, "And when the day of Pentecost was fully come, they were all with one accord in one place. And suddenly there came a sound from heaven as of a rushing mighty wind, and it filled all the house where they were sitting. And there appeared unto them cloven tongues like as of fire, and it sat upon each of them. And they were all filled with the Holy Ghost and began to speak with other tongues, as the Spirit gave them utterance."

As soon as I finished reading, I began to speak in tongues. God's word was truly living. God's word had manifested in me before my eyes. I was amazed and overwhelmed by God. I humbled myself completely and submitted to Him and His word. For I am His and He is mine. Years prior, I thought I missed my only moment. However,

God is the same yesterday, today, and forever. So you can always get a touch from God. We just have to be determined and push past whatever may be holding us back. Whether that's fear, doubt, our own insecurities, or the voices in our head, we have to push past it. Everything in this book is about getting that much closer to God. If we keep that the goal during the turbulences and trials life will throw at us, we'll keep our eyes on the prize—being *His.

One particular stormy night, I was heading from my apartment to my parents' home. What is normally about a ten-minute drive would soon turn into an excruciatingly long trip. The wind was slapping my sister and I as we ran to our cars while the rain smothered us. My sister was driving behind me as we headed out, and the sky was covered with dark clouds as the wind had my car shaking like a flag. The storm was so bad I actually began to panic a little while driving. I had both hands near the top of my steering wheel, and I was leaned up into the steering wheel, concentrating like a new sixteen-year-old driver. The rain and the wind were so bad at one point. I was unsure if we'd make it without having to pull over. I began to pray to God and ask Him for traveling mercies and for His protection over our lives. The more I prayed and the closer I got to my parents' house, the sky got brighter, and the storm grew weaker.

During your push in life, it will get better as long as you keep your eyes and heart set on God. By the time I got into the neighborhood, I was shaking because it had been that much of a traumatic car ride to get to that point. I continued praying, and then I noticed something. The sky was so much clearer in my parents' neighborhood, and the rain was letting up. By the time I pulled into my parents' driveway, the rain had completely stopped, and the sky was bright and beautiful. I broke down and cried at that moment. At that moment, I understood what God was showing me. The road may be tough, and we may become weary on this journey by walking out our faith and what we believe. However, we can't become weary in well doing. We have to trust that God has His hand on His child the whole way. We have to completely humble ourselves to Him and push past everything because the reward is great. The reward is God. Pushing past everything that will come at you in life won't be easy.

Everyone will go through different circumstances, but we must stay on course even if we can't see the end or what's next. Know that you are His and He is yours.

When my family lived in Spain, I was about five years old, and my sister and I were singing in the children's choir this particular Sunday. We had just begun singing the first song with everyone else, and suddenly, the power went out. As kids, initially, we all were scared because it was dark, and we couldn't see. Not only was it dark, but the equipment cut off also. Even though we were kids and we couldn't see at all, we knew enough to know that God was still in that place, and He used us. We paused for maybe a few seconds, and we began to sing again. We began to sing even though we couldn't see, even though the equipment had cut off. We truly pushed through. Do you trust God enough to push through?

On this journey, there will be times where you'll need to have *purposeful planning*. You will also always need to remember that God has placed a *unique umbrella* over your head and that your hedge of protection is vital to your walk. There will also be times of warfare where you'll need to look back on your *stamped seasons* and what God has already brought you through. And lastly, you'll always need to be *humbled* and understand it's because of Him that you are and because of Him that you can. Be like the kids in Spain and *push* past everything that will come your way, even if you can't see. For there is no devil in hell that can stop the plan the Lord has for you. You will do mighty things, you are mighty, you are set apart, you are a royal priesthood, a chosen people, a child of a King. You are *His.

Quotes

"Ignorance is the root of oppression and oppression is like a jar and ignorance is what keeps us trapped inside."

"If you're not sharing knowledge, you're spreading poison. Not moving forward is standing still, and standing still gets you nowhere."

"I'd rather be thought of by others as a fool for following my heart than to ignore my heart and look back and feel like a fool."

"Being silent is allowing the fire to burn. Just because you didn't cause it doesn't mean it's not affecting your environment."

"The life that you live reflects your true choice. For your mouth sings the music but your actions bleed ears with the truth."

"Everyone should see the world through the eyes of each generation. Once we understand those who came before us, those we stand with, and those who follow behind, we'll be a better world to see."

"Every situation has a silver lining. It's simply when the hopefulness of your heart shows up in tough situations."

"The acme of your life is now. Don't wait for a moment or look in the past for your best. Be your greatest you now."

"It's easy to do good when it's going good, but true authenticity is shown in the tough spots. It's about willpower."

"Don't allow your rubbernecking to slow everyone else down."

"Though the day may bring a lot your way, make sure you have a good headspace because, after all, you have the final say."

"A moment taken for granted is done by one with no noteworthiness on the magnitude of duration."

200 Up

A journey worth a thousand steps but as I look back, I'm only 200 up
This defeat I feel, I refuse to accept
Only God can get me out of this muck
This misery, this foolery, this tragedy
The circumstances defined
But with God on my side, I got the amnesty
The ups and downs of this life
Abase and abound, abase and abound
My flesh is down, and my crown hit the ground
But my spirit man stands strong and bold
My crown hit the ground good, I'm casting crowns
My world's not falling apart, it's falling into place as they'd say
No matter what I know, He's leading the way
I'm coming out of this quicksand
I'm down now, but a comeback is coming
But now I got anointing in this area
I'm walking into my next, no, I'm running
I promise to lead this generation, he said I dare you
It may not be pretty now, but there's purpose
I don't understand, but God I still trust you
All roads lead to my Piccadilly Circus
With every step back and set back, I'm packing on humility
Every hopeless night and lonely night, I'm tucking in patience
With every prayer I pray and amen I say, I'm
Building a warrior
Every step forward I take, I'm calling it a blessing
With every temporary setback, I'm calling it a lesson
I got a 1,000 lessons that account for my 200 blessings
I'm 200 up

What the Streets Say

I say I take up my cross and follow Christ daily
But what the streets say
Can the pavement testify
Will the trees sway in agreement?
Will the wind whistle in acknowledgment?
Does the mud take form of my footprints?
What the streets say
During the absence of light, somehow beneath my feet is shinning
Is there a light unto my path and lamp unto my feet?
Can the journey speak on the transformation?
Has it seen old things passed away and the new come?
What the streets say
Do the sunrays shine on me during my fight?
Does it see my battle and bloodshed?
Can it describe to you the fight within to kill this flesh?
Is there a repetitive denial to my freshly desire?
What the street says
Will the stop sign describe my halt?
The stillness in my body and me exalting the Lord
Will the green light tell you I'm making sure all the world will know?
Making disciples among nations
What the streets say
Will the clouds gloom and tell you how I lost my life for the Lord's sake?
And the sun comes out to explain how I found it in Him
Will the streets acknowledge the weight of the cross on your back?

Or will it witness you walking around with your "I am a fan" shirt?
What the streets say
"Then said Jesus unto his disciples, if any man will come after me, let
    him deny himself and take up his cross and follow me."

Juxtapose

I can't rap
But I have a message
I'm not a preacher
But there's a word inside of me
I don't have a platform
But I have an audience
I'm not the best public speaker
But I have something to say
I'm not a Victoria's Secret model
I'm not on the cover of *Vogue* magazine
But I can speak on beauty and tell you confidence comes from within
I didn't raise Lazarus from the dead
But I can tell you healing is in my hands
I don't have a degree or any awards
But I'm inferior to none
I wasn't raised in poverty
But my heart cries out for the poor
Though I walk through the valley of shadow of death
I will fear no evil
For His rod and His staff comfort me
We're a generation where we sound tough
We look like killers
We got mouths like sailors
We shun falling in love
We call virgins unicorns
We kill each other over colors
Or just because
But I'm telling you we're called to more

We got it all wrong
Trying to be a wolf
But we're called to be the sheep among the wolves
Lord, help us
Help us to be wise as serpents
And innocent as doves
I can't change the world
But I'll die trying
For, God, I'm yours, and I'll die about it, Lord
We murmur and complain
But we forget about the Israelites
Only to look up in confusion as to why we've only come and inch
I'm not a worship leader
But I'll change the atmosphere
I'm not Abraham
But the blessings on me
I'm a sinner, but my sins don't condemn me
I'm a good person
But at the gates, will Jesus say He knows me?

like there is no other real, and the world surrounds your catastrophe.
Well, what if I tell you your perception is skewed
That the true reality is not about you?
We seem so focused on the minuscule things that are right in front
    of us
That we stop and look at people like they aren't one of us,
Like they're up under us,
Like the better become fond of us
Because we're the only ones that can do wonderous.
I'm here to tell you that mindset is incorrect.
That you'll stay in the 4 × 4 box if you keep that mindset
That the world is infinite, and you stay stuck in that box
Until you look up from the thing you focus on and realize you've
    been missing a lot.

There are others with tragedies, others with dreams, others with disease, others with struggle, others with family, others with responsibilities, others with no hope, others with complete joy and peace.

There are other realities,

And until your reality affects their reality, reality is a 4 × 4 box that you're locked in

Soon to mean nothing when your fate is locked it.

And there ain't no coming back,

So let me help you get it right that 4 × 4 box should not be a life.

When you take off that lid and bust open the sides and use your life to affect other's life, now that's life.

No, that's living.

Your reality is your comparison to your perception of perfection

And until that perception is inclusive and not elusive, you'll be living exclusive.

And I'm thankful that's not my reality.

Coming to the realization that I'm alone,

What a revelation,

Not the part that I'm me or that no one else is.

But the part that no matter how hard I try, even in conversation,

No one else will ever be as with me than I can be.

Having this epiphany was like having a diagnosis.

It took me a long time to understand why my attempts to make my theories, desires, and reasonings stick with tape and glue was like I was in hypnosis,

Doing something I was told to do, trying to get on the same page with everyone else or at least help them see the book I was in.

Even those in the same book were never in the same chapter

And those few who did happen to pass through the chapter would never land on my page...how tragic

How can a lover of people, a leader of such be alone yet not alone?

Read this! Read this! As everyone turned the page...read this! I was yelling with my tape and glue.

Every now and then, people would tickle my fancy and turn to my page.

We would have shallow, deep conversations about the purpose of life
and money and how to make a difference in the world.

But soon enough, the glue didn't hold, and it was off to the next
pages…

Imagine my disappointment time and time again.

It's one thing to acknowledge a situation and another thing in its
entirety to embrace it

Learning to put the glue down and drop the tape was challenging,
but the part that was worse was not looking for something to
replace it.

The concept of being me, without anyone else, alone, specifically,
identifiably, originally, organically was foreign.

I never did that before.

Accepting that even if someone was on my page, they could never be
reading my line, on my word, enunciating my letter.

I know I'm fearfully and wonderfully made, but I had to learn that
being with myself is better than others being with me while I'm
not present.

Full Circle

I have a lot to say but don't know where to begin
The topics go so far east yet so far west
But ain't it funny how if you go so far west and so far east somehow, it'll meet
Everything goes full circle
What you were shown
What you heard
What you said
What you did produces a product
However, you always have a choice to be a product of your circumstances or not
It's a "fix your own meal or don't eat world" out there
You get nothing, but you can take all
Nothing's handed to you
Well, for the most of us
And now for the ignorance in our society, it has to vanish
I once tweeted,
"Ignorance is the root of oppression and oppression is like a jar and ignorance is what keeps us trapped inside."
It's very much true, and KeKe Palmer agreed because she retweeted it
I have a lot to say but few listeners
But that's okay
They say we've come so far
Yet at times one can turn around and be marching in the streets of Ferguson
I click on Facebook
I post about God
I get a few claps and an amen

But I can scroll down my timeline, and it's another video yelling,
    "World star!" with ten million views
I don't get it
I don't understand
Am I an old soul, or am I just a product of my upbringing
I don't even believe there's a such thing as an upbringing now
Just a friendship now because that's all they are bringing
We get loud, we cheer, we make the stadiums electric
But somehow, the church crowd is dead like someone pulled the plug
Well, maybe if you didn't go out the night before and in the club
    making love
I mean, fornicating, you'd have enough energy to give God some praise
But I'll leave that alone, for now, I don't want to leave somebody offended
We walk the streets of New York, Chicago, LA, DC, Atlanta, and
    your city
And we see the same homeless people every day
But we have yet to give a dime or even a God bless
Should I bring up the story of the good Samaritan
Or will you just hit me with the no one helped me excuses
Ain't it funny how doing what's right always has to be a fight
Many don't even gear up for the fight of living right
I declare it the world's most unpopular battle
Nowadays, everybody knows every rap,
Funny movie scene,
Kevin Hart's stand-up,
Classics, etc. from the past and present
It's even been jokingly said that if you can't finish
"In west Philadelphia born and raised"
That you ain't black
I know it's all fun and games
I agree
But how about if you can't finish
"For God so loved the world that He gave his only begotten son that
    whosoever believes in Him shall not perish but have everlasting life"
Then our society has failed
Everything in life goes full circle

Young and No Dumb

Waiting till we grow old to be wise for what?
Young and dumb no
Little experience a lot of mistakes, yes
Don't be defined by what the media says
Redefine your name
Don't let them claim that you'll be the same
Change the game
Re-proclaim your name
We stand between the past
We stand between the future
We are the present
I plead to the west coast
Down south
East coast
Up north
For the young people to come together and make a change
In the words of Michael Jackson
Lord rest his soul
"There comes a time when we heed to a certain call when the world
    must come together as one. There are people dying, and it's
    time to lend a hand to life, the greatest gift of all."
The plead is to the youth because power is in our hands
Destruction is in our hands
Envy is in our hands
Hate is in our hands

But change is in our hands
Influence is in our hands
A better society is in our hands
Now let's join hands and fight the fight they don't think we can come to
My distant friends in Baltimore looted Pennsylvania Avenue
My long distant neighbors looted the streets of West Florissant in
    Ferguson, Missouri
Young people
But young people chanted no justice, no peace, no justice, no peace
In the streets of New York, Ferguson, LA, Atlanta, Baltimore,
    Chicago, Florida, DC
And other cities by the thousands
Young people
I've said it once before one can chase a thousand, but two can put ten
    thousand to flight
It's biblical, but we have power in numbers
Never allow your mind to think a problem is too distant for you to
    make a change
Start your change in your community
In your household
On your job
In your church
On your streets
In your neighborhood and at your schools
As much as it is about Freddie Gray, Mike Brown, Trayvon Martin,
    Eric Garner, it's not
This is a message about unity and the power of people coming together
    as one
Call me ludicrous, but I believe unity can solve an awful lot of
    America's issues
But then again, I might just be ludicrous
I plead for leniency throughout our nation
Mercy unexpected
Mercy
Compassion or forgiveness shown toward someone
Blessed are the merciful

About the Author

Kayla Simmons is a motivational speaker and writer. She created the online community, The Baker Sisters, alongside her sister Valencia in 2015. The Baker Sisters is a community dedicated to millennials who love God.

In 1994, Kayla was born to Tahriq and Jenny Baker in Portsmouth, Virginia. She is the second of four children. Kayla, along with the rest of her siblings, has always had a desire to truly know God. Growing up, she journaled about any and everything she could think about. As a "military brat," Kayla has lived all over the United States and in various countries. She attended thirteen schools during her childhood and teenage years, and through those experiences, she has developed a unique worldview. In 2019, Kayla married Gregory Simmons, and they currently reside in Jacksonville, Florida.

Kayla has aspired to write a book since high school but never dreamed it would be possible. However, through God's timing and guidance, her dream has come to fruition. Kayla hopes that this book transforms the lives of everyone who reads it and motivates them to seek God in all they do.

Printed in the USA
CPSIA information can be obtained
at www.ICGtesting.com
LVHW010836070324
773597LV00015B/710

9 781649 522122